*Clement Freud's
Book of Hangovers*

Clement Freud's Book of Hangovers

Illustrated by Clive Francis

ELM TREE BOOKS . LONDON

First published in Great Britain 1981
by Sheldon Press, SPCK
First published in this edition 1986
by Elm Tree Books/Hamish Hamilton Ltd
27 Wrights Lane London W8 5TZ

Text copyright © 1981, 1986 by Clement Freud
Illustrations copyright © 1986 by Clive Francis

Research by Diana Pugh

British Library Cataloguing in Publication Data
Freud, Clement
   [Hangovers]. Clement Freud's book of
   hangovers.
   1. Alcohol — Physiological effect
   I. [Hangovers] II. Title
   641.8'74   QP801.A3
   ISBN 0-241-11856-5

Filmset by Pioneer, Perthshire
Printed in Great Britain by
Redwood Burn Ltd, Trowbridge, Wiltshire

For Dominic and Matthew
who saw how it was
and now know how it is

Contents

Acknowledgements

Thanks are due to the following for permission to quote from published material:

Buchanan Booth's Agencies Limited for extracts from *Booth's Handbook of Cocktails and Mixed Drinks* by John Doxat; Jonathan Cape Limited for extracts from *Other People* by Martin Amis and *On Drink* by Kingsley Amis; Ebury Press for the extract from *The Jeeves Cocktail Book* by Hugh Bredin; Faber and Faber Limited for the extracts from *The Fine Art of Mixing Drinks* by David Embury; Victor Gollancz Limited for the extract from *Lucky Jim* by Kingsley Amis; A. P. Watt Limited for the extract from 'Wine Water and Song' in *The Flying Inn* by G. K. Chesterton; and A. P. Watt Limited and Hutchinson Publishing Group Limited for the extract from 'Jeeves Takes Charge' in *Carry On Jeeves* by P. G. Wodehouse.

The author extends his grateful thanks to Diana Pugh whose inspired research and diligent proof-reading were absolutely invaluable.

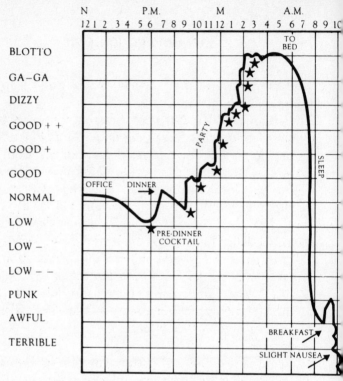

Based on the experience of a vast number of subjects the chart above is the result of a thorough analysis of many hangovers and its graph represents the average of this somewhat prevalent malady. A careful study will reveal the normal (although not exactly ideal) trend of the subject's physical condition for two hectic weekdays, to be chosen at will. Chart does not cover week-ends, which present a more difficult problem in fluctuation.)

To use the chart correctly, first follow directions closely beginning with 12 N, "NORMAL", and ending with 4 A.M., "BLOTTO". From here the hangover should check fairly accurately with the chart. If it does not, the wrong technique has been used. Some of the reasons for failure at this point are: (1) Slipping in a couple of straight ones at point 12 M. "GOOD + +". (2) Mixing drinks at 1 A.M. "DIZZY", and (3) Drinking inaccurately out of a bottle at 2 A.M. "GA-GA".

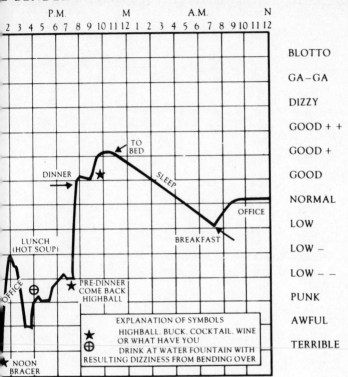

R CHART
E BENDER

	P.M.							M				A.M.						N	

2 3 4 5 6 7 8 9 10 11 12 1 2 3 4 5 6 7 8 9 10 11 12

BLOTTO

GA–GA

DIZZY

GOOD + +

GOOD +

GOOD

NORMAL

LOW

LOW –

LOW – –

PUNK

AWFUL

TERRIBLE

TO BED

DINNER

SLEEP

OFFICE

LUNCH (HOT SOUP)

BREAKFAST

PRE-DINNER COME BACK HIGHBALL

OFFICE

⊕

★

EXPLANATION OF SYMBOLS
★ HIGHBALL, BUCK, COCKTAIL, WINE OR WHAT HAVE YOU
⊕ DRINK AT WATER FOUNTAIN WITH RESULTING DIZZINESS FROM BENDING OVER

★ NOON BRACER

At the low point beginning at 8 A.M., "PUNK", the following should be borne in mind: (1) Breakfast at 8:15 A.M., "AWFUL", should consist only of tomato juice and the middle of a piece of dry toast. (2) At 10 A.M. "TERRIBLE", subject should under no circumstances eat caramels; and (3) The highball at 7 P.M., "LOW – –", should be a whiz.

When the hangover coincides with the chart, the chart should be referred to before going on a party so that emergencies and contingencies may be anticipated such as (1) Avoidance of brawls, (2) Running out of liquor, (3) When to do the least amount of work at the office and (4) Determining whether the physical condition will be "PUNK" or just "LOW – –" when the client calls to sign the contract.

(Chart courtesy of The Bailie Nicol Jarvie Hotel, Aberfoyle, Scotland.)

1

Hangovers

'Drunk' is when you have too much to drink. 'Hangover' is when some of you is sober enough to realise how drunk the rest of you is.

Push a drunk out of a first floor window and he will gather his bruised relaxed body from the pavement and make off for the neighbouring pub.

Do the same to a man with a hangover and you end up on a charge of murder.

When I was 23 years old I went to the south of France to continue my catering apprenticeship at an hotel in Cannes and the Managing Director who was very busy and spoke French very quickly asked to see me, shook my hand, bade me sit down, told me he hoped that I would be content, and that as a gesture to international co-operation between our countries I should drink a litre of wine per week with my meals, with his compliments, and good luck. He got up, I got up. I did not see him again for a month.

As I explained, he spoke quickly; I missed the 'per week' bit, had not at that time gone metric and was surprised when I ordered a litre of wine with my first lunch at the size of the bottle.

My colleagues looked on admiringly as I did my best for the old entente and finished it within the half hour lunch break. That night I had another litre and the next lunch and the next evening.

In those first weeks in Cannes I became the Captain of

the hotel football team though I played rugby; bought a second-hand motorbike with sidecar which I had no licence to drive; proposed marriage to several customers and the housekeeper who was 58, and on my twenty-fourth birthday won a substantial sum of money playing No. 24 in the casino. Throughout that time I moved in the oysterlight of an alcoholic haze, mistook customers for each other, gave people the wrong room keys, the wrong messages, the wrong bills, and quite often fell asleep behind the reception desk — but I never let down the generous Managing Director. That litre of wine was drunk twice a day, and on my day off I had lunch or dinner out and then returned to the hotel to claim my tipple.

At the end of the month I saw the Managing Director for the second time. He said, and he now spoke more slowly (or I understood him better), that the reports he had received about me were less than totally satisfactory.

'It appears', he said, 'that you drink.'

'Only', I answered, 'what you so kindly asked me to drink for the sake of national amity.' Indeed, I assured him, there was little opportunity after that to consume other liquor, and I promised him that I had not done so.

'But you drink *two litres a day*' he said, looking at his notes.

'With your compliments' I said, belching gently and trying to get him into focus.

'I offered you one litre a week.'

There was not a lot I could say. My casino winnings went to pay my wine bills and Cannes took on an entirely new appearance — not just because it was spring. Customers emerged from their cocoons of anonimity; keys achieved an identity. The Croisette outside remained static when it had previously refused to settle down, and my eyes returned

3

to the colour specified on page two of my passport signed by Ernest Bevin.

I have been interested in hangovers ever since.

How it all began

Some 10,000 years ago primitive man began to abandon his habit of wandering around in small groups, slaughtering passing dinosaurs and eating them on the spot. Primitive man Mark II settled in one place, reared animals and grew crops in a stable environment.

After this, allow a few hundred years for man to discover that if he left certain fruit, or honey and water, to stand in a warm atmosphere, there was a definite change in taste; if consumed in quantity there were interesting after-effects, initially pleasant, later less agreeable. You now have an approximate date for the invention of alcohol. The first hangover occurred about three-and-a-half hours later. The location of this event is not easy to pin-point, but as the species of vine which grows wine grapes is a native of Persia, there is a school of thought that lays it all squarely at the Persians' door. This must come as a considerable blow to the Ayatollah.

The next important discovery was that there were those who could drink significantly more than others without falling over. Others yet, who fell over readily, managed to get up more quickly and more joyfully than their colleagues. Since then nothing much has changed but people have talked about it a lot.

Darius I, King of the Persians in the first century BC wrote as his own epitaph, *Darius could drink any quantity of wine without being inebriated.* It was the first recorded drinking boast. Around him, courtiers who had tried to

prove him wrong sat in silent anguish waiting for the world to stop turning — and this was many centuries before anyone suspected that the earth actually turned of its own volition. Hangovers have progressed from those simple beginnings.

In translation

The word hangover came into usage at the turn of this century via America. In view of the general sympathy aroused by the hangover in foreign parts, a glossary of the word in other languages might be useful.

Country	Word	Translation
Spain	Resaca	Malady

Italy	Malessere	Malady
	Malessere dopo una sbornia	Malady after a booze-up
France	Gueule de bois	Wooden throat — should be said with a throaty cough and a shrug.
Denmark	Tømmermaend	Carpenters
Norway	Bockrus	After effect, kick back
Sweden	Baksmalla	After effect, kick back
Netherlands	Kater	Cat

Germany	Katzenjammer	Wailing of cats
Poland	Kociokwik	Wailing of kittens
	'Kac' if substantial	Cat

Russia — no official recognition of hangovers by order of Supreme Soviet, but hangovers are alive and well and known as pokhmel'e. Australians call it 'a mouth like the bottom of a cocky's cage'. Countries not listed above understand mime based on bloodshot eyes, sloth and general disorientation.

Social class

Attitudes to hangovers vary significantly with social class; cures tend to be very much more readily available in the West End of London than in the English suburbs or provinces. Ask a Hackney chemist to make you up something for a hangover and you get a packet of Alka Seltzer and an unsympathetic grin. Try it in a St. James' chemist and you will be on the receiving end of considerable concern and a restorative draught (retailing at £1.70 a small bottle) which will keep you going until the bar at the Ritz Hotel opens.

The most famous of the remedies of the Twenties, heyday of the hangover, was dispensed at Mr. Perkins' Chemist Shop in Piccadilly and known as Perkins' Green Flash — the name conjuring up sunsets on P. and O. liners tinged by pink gins. Sadly Perkins is now a gift shop and the last dispenser of the Flash declined to disclose the formula which he will doubtless take to his sober grave. The ingredients, he muttered as he bade me farewell, have become 'unobtainable'.

The general attitude to hangovers then is complicated by considerations of nationality, morality, politics and class — especially class. The working class victim gets very little sympathy on the No. 12 bus to the factory gates; the banker is shown understanding and envy by his colleagues, which is all the stranger because the manual worker will not work that much less well on the morning after, while the hungover banker's creative output is likely to be nil.

The English butler

This might be a moment to reflect on the English butler, a character who comes into his own with a hangover. The modulated speech of the Jeeves' of this world was rehearsed with the hangover in mind. Butler schools spend much of the first month quietening down the every action of the gentlemen's gentleman, from the soft-shoe approach to the placing of a napkin on the saucer of the coffee-cup to silence the unseemly clatter of spoon on china.

Perhaps the *perfect* butler will ensure that your stomach is properly lined before you start to imbibe, but he must also be ready with an emergency post-imbibing restorative. Jeeves, you may recall, was engaged on the strength of his hangover cure. He first enters Bertie Wooster's life one jaded weekday morning; assessing the situation at a glance, he found his way to the kitchen and returned bearing a glass:

> 'If you would drink this, sir,' he said, with a kind of bedside manner rather like a royal doctor shooting the bracer into the sick prince. 'It is a little preparation of my own invention. It is the Worcester sauce that gives it its colour. The raw egg makes it nutritious. The red

pepper gives it its bite. Gentlemen have told me they have found it extremely invigorating after a late evening.'

I would have clutched at anything that looked like a lifeline that morning. I swallowed the stuff. For a moment I felt as if somebody had touched off a bomb inside the old bean and was strolling down my throat

*with a lighted torch, then everything seemed suddenly
to get all right. The sun shone in through the window;
birds twittered in the tree-tops; and, generally speaking,
hope dawned once more . . .*

P. G. Wodehouse: Jeeves Takes Charge

The Final Test

If you can still lie on the floor without holding on to
anything you are not really drunk.

2

Know your enemy

. . . Oh, I've had the lot, I admit it, Mary. Methylated spirits.
Turpentine. After-shave. The lot. Silver-polish. Weed-killer.
Paint-remover. Washing-up liquid. Everything. Disinfectant.
4711. Cough-mixture. Nasal decongestant. Windolene.
Optrex. I've had them all.

Martin Amis *Other People*

There are those who genuinely believe that they cannot
come to terms with a problem without knowing all about it.
This chapter is for them. Those who feel that knowledge of
the truth would mean the end of all enjoyment of drink are
advised to turn to the section entitled 'Know your drink'.
This is pretty depressing too, but not quite as much. The
principal symptoms of the hangover are:

Dehydration

Alcohol in quantity depresses the brain, which is actually
why most people drink it. Alcohol first depresses the parts
of the brain that control inhibitions, leaving a feeling of
temporary wellbeing and self-confidence, but the brain
controls the production of a useful commodity known as
A.D.H. or Anti-Diuretic Hormone. When the brain is slowed
down by alcohol, less A.D.H. is produced, and the more
you drink the more quickly you get rid of fluids. Hence the

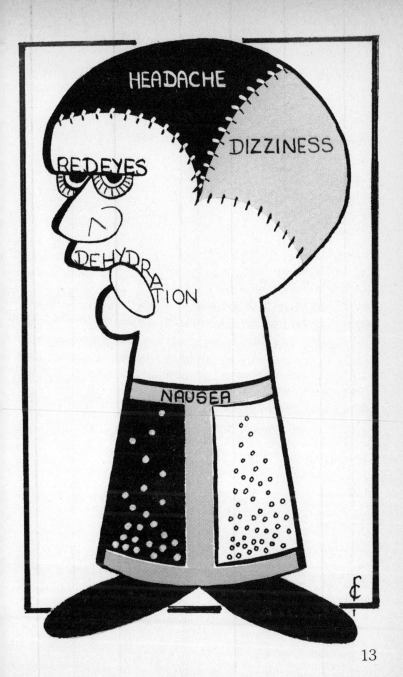

13

dehydration. Lack of fluid causes a variety of different disturbances all through the body's mechanism, and it follows that most of the other symptoms of a hangover are indirectly caused by dehydration. A determined attempt to combat this by drinking water, milk or fruit juice before, during and immediately after drinking alcohol is therefore a satisfactory way of dealing with a hangover.

Headache

A headache is one of the effects of dehydration and can also be caused by toxic substances known as congeners in the drink itself. Some drinks have more congeners than others; vodka is low, port and brandy tend to be high, increasing the headache in proportion. Personal chemistry also affects the body's reaction to different types of congeners, which is why some drinks suit some people better than others, irrespective of the amount of congeners in the drink.

Paracetemol is probably better than aspirin for a hangover headache; aspirin can irritate the stomach and will make the situation worse.

Red Eyes

A minor but irritating complaint, which has the added disadvantage of being very difficult to disguise; dark glasses are a dead give-away. The eye is surrounded by fluid and with the depletion of this fluid, the blood vessels in the eye expand and the eye becomes bloodshot.

Dizziness

Alcohol causes an increased flow of blood to the head, affecting the central nervous system and the mechanism of the inner ear which controls balance. This causes what Lord Byron describes as 'vertiginousness', usually only when the victim is actually drunk, but sometimes after the alcohol has left the body.

The gastric consequences of a hangover are usually explained away vaguely as the result of 'acidity'. It is not quite as simple as that. The stomach's reaction to taking anything in, be it Weetabix, water, whisky or Windolene, is to produce more acid to deal with the substance entering the stomach. The level of acid in the body overall is described as the pH factor, and is measured on a scale of 1-14. The usual body level is about 7.4. Dehydration, which lowers the normal level of water in the body cells and upsets the cellular balance of water and salts, changes the pH level, and this affects the rate of *all chemical reactions throughout the body*. We shall not pursue the pH factor any further, but it does explain why the ills of a hangover appear at the time to be so devastatingly widespread.

The medical attitudes to cures intended to correct the acid imbalance with alkaline preparations is not encouraging. The balance adjusts itself in time, but any attempt to speed up the process by taking large quantities of bicarbonate of soda or patent antacid preparations brings only psychological relief; there is no way that one can take in enough alkali to effect an instant improvement.

Bearing this in mind, it may be better to take the advice given by Kingsley Amis in his book *On Drink*, and take acid instead, in the form of unsweetened fruit juice, grapefruit or even vinegar:

The reasoning behind this, known as Philip Hope-Wallace's syndrome, is that your stomach, on receiving a further dose of acid, will say to itself, 'Oh, I see, we need more alkaline', and proceed to neutralise itself. Bicarbonate of soda will make it say, 'Oh I see, we need more acid', and do you further damage.

"The mixture turned black and gave off smoke."

Kingsley Amis tells of a time when he took vodka as a chaser for bicarbonate. His friend said 'Let's see what is happening in your stomach', and poured the remnant of the vodka into what was left of the bicarbonate. The mixture turned black and gave off smoke.

This story has not been disproved in print, mainly because we are too mean to waste vodka. For the record Amis is wrong. Had there been a little prussic acid in the receptacle used for the experiment it could have happened.

3

Know your drink

'I rather like bad wine ... one gets so bored with good wine.'
Benjamin Disraeli

Disraeli was a Conservative whose considerable talents were assisted by a very considerable amount of luck. The luck included a certain immunity to hangovers.

The claim that good wine causes less severe hangovers than bad is one that contains an irritating amount of truth. Cheap wines of dubious origins are likely to contain more vicious congeners than their more carefully produced competitors.

Congeners cause hangovers and it is well to remember that brandy, whisky, port, sherry, vermouths, rums, (especially dark rums) and red wine, particularly rich and heavy ones, contain a good many. This leaves Gin, Vodka and Bacardi on which to make satisfactory inroads, with still dry white wine as an each-way hedge. Individual reaction to congeners varies, which is why some people get worse hangovers after drinking the same quantity and quality of booze as others.

Bubbly and the like

The bubbles in wine (champagne, sparkling moselle etc.) speed up the rate at which alcohol enters the bloodstream and make you drunker faster. The high acidity of these

19

'I rather like bad wine . . . one gets so bored with good wine.'
Benjamin Disraeli

wines, like brut champagne, also intensifies the resultant hangover.

Hangovers induced by champagne tend to include deep depression as a constituent. There is no medical reason for this but much psychological data, mainly arising from the celebratory aspect of champagne which makes the ensuing 'downer' that much more of a contrast.

Beware of tonic water; saccharin-based minerals taken with spirits speed up the absorption rate of the alcohol. There are people who blame the quinine, but this is less than fair when you have accompanied two baby tonics with four large vodkas.

Even the little woman who sticks to sherry before, and a teensy glass of port after a meal, is actually consuming more congener-rich alcohol than her boorish beer-swilling man. An average glass of port deposits more alcohol in the bloodstream than a pint of strong lager. Men in search of companionship after the office party should shun the giggly sherry girls and go for the solemn auntie figure who consoled herself with neat vodka. Not only will she be more grateful; she will drive you home more safely and be less irritable in the morning. Avoid liberated females who seem to be obsessed with the *right* of women to suffer from hangovers.

4

Know yourself

I had, in my drinking days in France, a friend who tried hard to make me join the better class gatherings of the Riviera. He painted, I cooked: we were both very poor. Like me he drank red wine and dreamt of golden coloured whisky, even whiskey (the letter 'e' between k and y denotes that it comes from some other land than Scot).

Olive oil

At that time, 1948, opportunities to drink hard liquor were few and far between. One day, after an especially long pause, I received a message about a party in the square at Antibes. An English yacht-owner was celebrating the re-marriage of his ex-wife, and had taken over the Café des Anglais, and my friend, who knew the tycoon, had got me an invitation to attend. 'Come and call for me at my studio and we'll prepare for the evening' he wrote. 'Be there at 5 p.m.'

I arrived punctually. He welcomed me with conspiratorial glee, and told me it was going to be just like going to the Savoy without the bill. I followed him to his kitchen, he ceremoniously got two large port glasses and a bottle of olive oil and said 'This lines the stomach; it is not going to be very nice but by God, we'll drink the rest of them under the table. Gulp this down and we shall be the only three-bottle men in the Alpes Maritimes.'

The party was due to start at 6 o'clock and so as not to appear over-eager we determined to delay our arrival until 6.05; the square at Antibes was fifteen minutes fast walk. As there was nothing in the house to take away the taste of the oil before we fell on the whisky, we played a little backgammon and at 5.49 p.m. emptied our glasses, gave each other the amazed looks that pass between olive oil drinkers and trotted out into the evening.

It all went according to plan. We reached Le Café des Anglais at 6.05 and flashed our invitation card. 'Alors,' said the Propriètaire, 'that party was last night.'

My friend pawned his watch and we went to Le Café Marseillaise where the whisky was cheaper.

The writer of a sixteenth-century recipe for 'Sallet Oyle' — to be taken with new milk — adds gloomily 'But howe sicke you will be with the preuntion I will not heere determine'.

Goodness, I know what he meant.

Good cheer

Here are a few truths, and remember they are only for those who want the best of both worlds, to drink and be of good cheer afterwards.

1 *Drink causes hangovers but less drink causes lesser hangovers.*

   My advice is to drink slowly, dilute your drink and use small glasses such as the Japanese use for saki. If you go to Japan you cannot help noticing that all the same, the poor dears get terribly drunk on the minuscule glasses they use.

2 Sweet drinks act faster than dry ones, iced ones more quickly than those at room temperature, hot ones have an instant effect which lasts a shorter time. To put it another way, they all get you in the end.

Alcohol *leaves* the system at around a single measure of spirits, of half a pint of beer or cider an hour, and the stomach cannot, even when bombarded with fruit juice, water of black coffee, significantly speed up the process. Attempts to time your consumption to avoid hangovers will lead to severe depression.

3 *Drink dehydrates.*
Remember that most of the physical ills of a hangover are due, directly or indirectly, to dehydration. The advice to 'take more water with it', usually delivered when a man is actually on the floor, has a higher irritant potential than any phrase except 'I told you so', but drinking soft drinks in the intervals of hard one does help.

4 *'You can tell a man who boozes by the company he chooses.'*
Guilt plays a large part in hangover misery, and guilt is caused as much by vague recollections of what nearly happened than by actual deeds. When planning to drink too much, try to do so in the immediate vicinity of people whom you are unlikely to see again. This will cause a physical rather than a mental hangover, which is much easier to treat.

5

Kill or cure

There comes a time in every serious hangover when the victim believes and usually says, that only death can put a satisfactory end to his suffering. While I do not deny that death is the ultimate cure, (death being nature's way of telling you to slow down) it is messy, final, and often causes unnecessary suffering to those of the drinker's nearest and dearest whom he has not already mortally offended during the pre-hangover proceedings. The choice of a cure depends upon whether one believes that it should:

a) dispel all desire to drink alcohol again, or
b) restore the patient to a state where he can contemplate the next drink with equanimity.

The ancient Greeks

Pliny, who is no longer available for comment, wrote 'Let a man drink of the Lake of Clitorius, he shall take a misliking and a loathing for wine'. The Greek Tourist Board keeps pretty quiet about the exact location of the healing waters, but for many people unused to resinated wines, the first heavy evening on retsina or ouzo can produce similar effects. For those unable to take a trip to the Lake of Clitorius, the ancient Greeks had several other aversion cures, including:

Eggs of a night-owl in wine (Pliny)

A mullet killed in red wine (Pliny)
Two eels, suffocated in wine (Pliny)
A lion's sternum, taken in wine (Albertus Magnus)
The essence of the Sarmentis (a kind of twig) given to
   the victim without his knowledge (Democritus)

Interestingly, although alleged to create an aversion, all but one of these remedies are designed to be taken in *wine*.

It would be more accurate to describe them as distinctively flavoured hairs of the dog.

Aversion cures

The cures above, with the exception of Democritus' twig, were voluntary remedies; aversion cures imposed by higher authority tended to be more drastic, but effective in that they deterred the recipient from courting further hangovers. The first Sultan Suliman was known to order molten lead to be poured down the throats of persistent drunkards; Lycurgus of Sparta decreed that their legs be broken. The 'Drunkards Chair', described by a sixteenth century historian, Olaus Magnus, exposed imbibers to the more subtle punishment of painful ridicule. The victim was made to sit, clutching a horn of ale, in a sharp-pointed seat suspended on ropes and pulleys, while his jeering companions pulled on the rope to bump the seat up and down on the floor.

Enterprising burghers of the Newcastle Corporation in the sixteenth century invented the Newcastle Jacket, made of a wine barrel with one end knocked out. The offender's head was placed through a hole cut in the other end and he was forced to parade himself and his hangover through the streets of the town like a man in a circular sandwich board.

American cures

Later cures designed to wean the patient from drink were generally designed for alcoholics rather than hangover victims but some substances, such as Peruvian bark (cinchona rubra) were used for both. Its near relation

29

quinine is still a popular constituent of 'hangover mixtures'. In the quantities prescribed by Dr. D'Unger, who used it with considerable success on both sides of the Atlantic, the cure probably worked because after a few days of the treatment the patient would swear to give up drink (or anything else) provided he could give up the bark as well.

> *1 lb cinchona rubra, soaked in 1 pint diluted alcohol. Strain it, and evaporate down to half a pint. Administer to the patient 1 teaspoonful every three hours, and occasionally moisten his tongue between the doses the first and second days. It acts like quinine. The patient can tell by a headache if he is getting too much.*
>
> Drunkenness Cured *(1880)*

Another nineteenth century American, one Dr. Jarvis, designed a more palatable remedy intended, like the Peruvian Bark cure, to create an aversion for alcohol. He believed the craving for liquor was induced by a shortage of potassium in the system and that honey, which contains potassium, would reduce the patient's desire to drink. Six teaspoonsful of honey were prescribed at twenty-minute intervals, on the first day. The next morning, six teaspoonsful of honey are given before the breakfast boiled egg, and six more ten minutes after the patient has eaten it. By lunchtime the dose is down to four teaspoons accompanied by a glass of tomato juice, a portion of chopped beef and four more teaspoonsful of honey after the meal. Dr. Jarvis may have been over-optimistic in his instruction to leave the whisky bottle beside the patient at all times because 'it probably will not be drunk', but his cure would undoubtedly alleviate a hangover. Honey contains fructose — fruit syrup which

helps the body rid itself of alcohol — and helps top up the blood sugar level, which is generally low the morning after a late night.

Masochistic cures

At one remove from the aversion cure is the masochistic cure. This gives the victim a chance to sublimate any guilt feelings by subjecting himself to a really nasty experience. Liquid cures of this type owe much of their effectiveness to the popular belief that anything that tastes really disgusting must of course do you good. The latter misconception is one that has kept doctors, nannies, British restaurants, and chemists in business for years and, unkind detractors might add, the manufacturers of Underberg and Fernet Branca too. Why not increase the agony by making up for yourself a genuine eighteenth century 'Surfeit-Water'; the price of the necessary three and a half gallons of 'proof spirits' alone should provide a salutary shock to the system.

> *Take Centuary, Marigold-flowers, Mint, Rosemary, Mugwort, Scordium, Rue, Carduus, Balm, Dragons, St. John's wort, each two handfuls; roots of Angelica, Butter-bur, Piony, Scorzerona, each seven ounces; Calamus Aromaticus, Galginal, Angelica-seeds, Cara-ways, each ten drachms, Ginger six drachms, red Poppy-flowers three handfuls; proof-spirits three gallons; water one gallon and a half; macerate, distil and dulcify with fine sugar, one pound and a half for use.*
>
> George Smith A Compleat Body of Distilling *(1738)*

A cheaper, but no less nasty, thrill can be obtained by following the advice of an Anglo-Saxon sage, who advised:

> *Whenever thou drinkest ale, take earth's strength as antidote, for earth acts against ale.*

Spontaneous combustion

No study of aversion cures would be complete without a mention of one rumour assiduously cultivated and documented with a wealth of pseudo-scientific detail in nineteenth century books on the effects of alcohol. I used to think that Krook, the rag and bone dealer in *Bleak House* who dies of spontaneous combustion, was the product of Dickens' own imagination, and was astonished to find that spontaneous combustion as a result of too much alcohol was actually considered seriously as a scientific phenomenon. One suspects that the popularity of the theory implies a certain amount of wishful thinking on the part of the Temperance Movement, but the propaganda may have averted a few hangovers by dissuading the late-night reveller from taking a last night-cap before retiring.

'The fatty degeneracy of the structure may be so extensive, and the soaking of the entire frame in unchanged alcohol so thorough, as to render the man dangerously prone to a most lamentable consummation from a common outward cause, his alcohol proving an aptitude for combustion in a way he little dreamt of. Falling asleep near a fire or candle, a spark lights upon him, and having become as it were a compound of an oil or spirit lamp, with a dash of phosphorus to boot, he burns with a strange burning, producing little flame or heat, but steadily consuming away in horrid stench, leaving but a small residue of dark, offensive, unctuous dross to mark the place where he lay.'
(Professor James Miller, nineteenth-century writer on alcoholism)

The Irish Solution

An Irishman poured two bottles of Guinness down the loo each evening so that he didn't have to drink during the night.

6

Classic cures

So much has been written, so inaccurately, about the orgies of the ancient world that the casual reader might be forgiven for wondering when the Greek philosophers were sober enough to string two words together, or how Julius Caesar summoned the energy to cross the Alps, let alone invade Britain. Nevertheless the civilisation responsible for the orgy as we know it, was also the birthplace of the hangover cure; a substantial number of the remedies used by later generations of jaded debauchees have a respectable classical pedigree.

Watering the wine

The Greeks had a sensible approach to alcohol. They considered drinking a pleasure, drunkenness followed by hangovers a bore. The golden rule was to be careful about what they drank. Wine was diluted with water in a proportion of about 2:5. (Writers and other feckless parasites were said to reverse the proportions.) Dilution reduced the alcoholic content and minimised the problem of dehydration. The blending of the various wines with water to make a suitable festive mixture was a task which needed great care, and before a feast a 'chairman' was chosen to be responsible for the mixing. Socrates was a popular host because he was considered a connoisseur of wine and an experienced blender. He also preferred small drinking-vessels to keep consumption down. The drinking of unmixed wine was regarded as foolish and in bad taste; a practice fit only for barbarian tribes such as the Belgae and the Celts. They shared this sentiment with the Old Testament writer of the Book of Proverbs: 'Wisdom', he wrote 'hath mingled her wine'.

Wine and cheese

Wine was flavoured with other ingredients supposed to prevent it from causing intoxication; ginger and pepper were the most popular of the various spices used, and grated cheese was a common addition. Not, perhaps, an especially attractive mixture by modern standards, but palatable enough when compared with other surviving recipes for ancient Greek food and drink. The idea of cheese as a preventive against the ill-effects of wine continued certainly until the late middle ages, and they are still served together. Aficianados of wine and cheese evenings, though few, realise the original reason for the custom.

Romans used to retire to be sick in the middle of banquets — a drastic but effective method of preventing a hangover the next day — but since both Greeks and Romans frequently added resin, vinegar and sea-water to the festive draught this is hardly surprising. The habit of swallowing vinegar to cure drunkenness continued well into the nineteenth century.

Avoid the fumes

The Greeks believed intoxication was caused primarily by

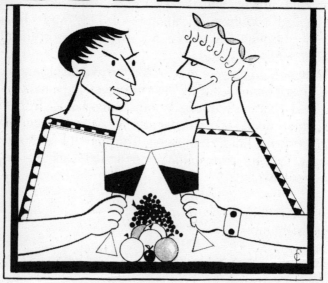

noxious fumes from the wine rising to the brain, and they used special ointments to keep these fumes at bay. The poet Horace when inviting Virgil to dine at his house, tells him not to forget his anti-fume remedy. All were agreed too, on the beneficial effects of wreaths worn for drinking. At first these were plain wooden fillets, but later they were made with plants believed to have special medicinal properties. Violets, myrtle and roses were the favourites, but ivy and cabbage leaves were also popular and made a nice change from all that boring laurel. Just to be on the safe side they sometimes decorated the wine-jars with wreaths to nullify the fumes at source and the competitors in drinking contests wore wreaths strategically placed around the body. There are some who believe that when Alexander the Great dropped dead during such a contest it was due to his ruthlessness.

Dressing to drink

It was important to select the correct costume for drinking; amethyst was thought to counteract the fumes best; and amethyst-coloured robes and amethyst jewellery guaranteed an evening free from disagreeable consequences. Amethyst-studded drinking cups had a long vogue until the reign of Nero (68-54 B.C.), who had an aversion to amethysts.

Bitter almonds rather than the usual sweet variety were taken before feasts, presumably with the idea that, being rich in oil, they lined the stomach. The appeal of powdered pumice stone dissolved in water before a drinking bout understandably failed to maintain its appeal after the eruption of Vesuvius on Pompeii in 79 AD.

The Hair of the Dog

Despite the care they took with hangover prevention, drinkers of the ancient world frequently also needed a cure.

> *Take the hair, it is well written,*
> *Of the dog by whom you're bitten.*
> *Work off one wine by his brother,*
> *And one labour with another.*

The Egyptians were the first to use cabbage as both a preventative and a cure. Aristotle was loud in its praises, especially as a remedy for hangover headache, and Athenaeus of Naucratis, who pontificated on nearly everything like a former day Eric Heffer, wrote:

> *Last evening you were drinking deep,*
> *So now your head aches. Go to sleep;*
> *Take some boiled cabbage when you wake*
> *And there's an end of your headache.*

It may be no coincidence that sauerkraut is still a favourite food among Germans and other nations where teetotalism is comparatively rare.

Drunkards soup

The poet Horace, who was more of a 'Giscard' figure, recommends African snails and roasted onions to restore the jaded palate. The French clearly took his advice to heart; snails are the traditional dish of the wine-growing districts and the Parisians still swear by Drunkards Soup, which was until quite recently available to home-going

revellers at the cafés of Les Halles which did for Paris Society what Covent Garden Pubs used to do for London night clubbers. The ingredients are one pound of onions, sliced very thinly. Half a pound of butter in which you simmer the onions until they are soft. A bottle of champagne which you pour onto the buttery onions, whereafter you decant all into a soup tureen, cover it with a well scraped Camembert cheese which forms a lid, sprinkle a few toasted breadcrumbs over the cheese and bake the tureen in a medium oven until the cheese has melted and the crumbs

39

crisped. For each portion, put a slice of lid into a soup-bowl and anoint it with the alcoholic soup. Freshly ground pepper, even cayenne, may be needed as accompaniment, no salt, salt and champagne make poor bedfellows.

Fruit and fish

Pliny explains that apples, quinces and pears act on a hangover by 'repressing vapours flying up into the head causing distemperature of the brain as (in) a surfeit of wine or strong drink'.

The Greeks had inadvertently discovered the properties of fructose, one of the few things that even modern medical opinion actually admits to be of benefit in curing a hangover.

Fish is reputedly good for the brain in sickness as well as in health — particularly, it seems, the herring. In Germany and some Scandinavian countries, soused herrings are combined with raw onions and sour cream or yoghurt as a 'morning-after' dish; the phrase 'he needs a herring' is a German euphemism to describe a man with a hangover. The herring was appreciated in England too; judging by the frequent references to them made by Sir John Falstaff, Sir Toby Belch and their companions, they were eaten by drinkers in the Elizabethan era, although they have lost popularity as a hangover food today.

Eggs

Long before the discovery of the Prairie Oyster, the second-century Greek physician and philosopher Galen wrote in praise of eggs as a cure for what the Irish describe as a 'sick stomach'. He recommended them lightly boiled, which may be some consolation to those who feel that people who can face raw eggs in such a state have no business to complain of a hangover at all. Egg possets and caudles — hot drinks of milk or gruel curdled with ale or wine — were dispensed to delicate revellers well on into the eighteenth century, but it does not seem to be until the early 1900s that some enterprising American barman, baulked of the real oysters which became prized as a cure-all once they became rare and expensive, had the brilliant idea of combining raw egg-yolks and Worcestershire sauce.

H_2O and all that

Water taken internally or applied externally is a good corrective. As your average lush is distrustful of water (W. C. Fields 'I never drink water; fish fuck in it') advising physicians have felt it tactful to mitigate the full horror of *aqua pura* by suggesting harmless additives. In Russia they prescribe black bread soaked in water for hangovers. (Black bread cleanses the breath). They also provide black bread and water for their prisoners but this may be unconnected with the subject matter in hand. Persius advises a quick plunge into the River Tiber to expunge the fumes of the previous night's revelries. Take no heed of this. The Roman sewerage system disgorged untreated effluent directly into the river through the Cloaca Maxima, so the bath may not have been as beneficial as he believed. (Beware also the waters of Liverpool, the quality of Mersey is strained.)

Externally, hot water provokes a healthy sweat; hot baths are exceedingly beneficial and hot towels around the head have helped many a poor politician to compose a more sensible speech than his condition warranted. The

'I never drink water; fish fuck in it'

traditional Roman accompaniment to hot towels upon the brow, iced water upon the genitals, is now out of fashion — except in Japan where it is available under the heading Special Service.

Galen the Greek wrote a lot about relieving hangovers. He advocated the application of hot fomentations to the head, friction massage with unguents, and wrapping the brow in cabbage leaves. After this, he recommended drinking barley or wheat-water with a meal of eggs, lettuce and other juicy herbs, lentil-water and pease-pudding. The aim was to induce sleep; if it failed the patient should have a hot bath or shower. I suspect that Galen secretly admitted that the only real cure for a hangover is the passage of time and so offered these suggestions as a means of passing through this period as pleasantly as possible. However, there is no reason why a version of this treatment (suitably modified to cater for individual requirements) should not be tried at home with the aid of a co-operative friend. For those who are temporarily friendless but in funds, about £20 a head, excluding the pease-pudding and cabbage leaves, will secure similar service in a respectable massage parlour — if that is not a contradiction in terms.

Saunas

Were I versed in the logistics of health I would be able to write with authority about the effects of steam baths and massage upon a hungover disposition; let it suffice that I write with feeling and experience. I know as much about steam baths and massage as most, having once been engaged by a magazine — long since deceased — to survey such establishments, I followed this up by doing a series on health resorts, and became a twelve stone jockey, when

God had intended me to weigh-in at around two stone more. Whatever anyone tells you, a sauna does less for a hangover than the makers of the sauna claim. It causes you to sweat, which causes you to have a thirst, which causes you to drink, which is what gave you the hangover in the first place and took you into the sauna.

Massage

A massage is a fractionally better idea. If the massage is given by a Japanese woman who walks up and down your spine it makes you grimly determined not to do it again. A masseur or -euse tends to make you hold in your stomach, brace your muscles, pretend that your condition is better than it is, and for a hangover that is exactly the discipline you should have had in mind. Tension is relaxed by massage, causing you to realise how drunk you were, how awful you feel, and how badly you need a drink.

On the outskirts of Helsinki there is an hotel with a dozen sauna suites where I stayed during a SALT conference. I went to the sort of dinner where people make monosyllabic remarks after which everyone holds the glass by their fourth waistcoat button, looks into the middle distance and drains the contents. I ended up in a sauna suite with a Norwegian defence attaché; he said that we should have gone to a nightclub if only we had been able to walk. The suite contained a sauna, a sitting-room with a bar, a slab for massage, a french window that gave onto a snow covered slope, and a woman so sensationally plain that one's entire attention could be focused on the treatment. We kept our hangovers at bay by saunas, rolling in the snow, drinking vodka and being massaged by the woman who looked not

just as if she had run into a bus, but as if someone had held her hard into the side of the bus while it drove past.

Perhaps massage was not always like this: it might be that steam baths have a different effect than does dry heat. What is certain is that when in agony, doing something is better than letting the full after-effects of the hangover consume your every thought.

Brewer's droop

One of the most troublesome side effects of the demon drink is that, in the words of the porter in Macbeth, 'it provokes the desire but it takes away the performance'. The classic remedy for this is to burn together the liver of a frog and a hedgehog, place the ashes in a bag and carry this around the person so as not to be embarrassed by impotence at awkward moments. By the late eighteenth century, due to one thing and another, including the national shortage of hedgehogs, strychnine was offered as a substitute. This can be effective, provided that you bear in mind that a little strychnine goes a long way and a lot lands you at the Assizes.

7

Sterner stuff

Samuel Pepys, who much enjoyed a glass or three of wine between dalliance and the clap, rarely complained of anything worse than a headache upon the morning after. The 'morning draught' which he took to revive himself was probably a kind of purl-ale or purging-ale. A popular recipe for this flavoured ale included senna, coriander seeds, rosemary and sage-flowers, but the senna was often (perhaps wisely) omitted and other herbs substituted. In

1692 Robert Boyle, a friend and contemporary of Pepys, proposed green hemlock inserted into the socks as a serious cure for the after-drinking 'heid-ake', and Pepys himself advocated betony leaves, either chewed or held in the hand, 'to keep a feeble brain from drunkenness'.

Fortified wines

By the turn of the century however, certain plans were afoot which were to change the whole face of the hangover. In 1703, the year of Pepys' death, the Methuen Treaty was signed with Portugal. This resulted in a system of import duties favouring the wines of Portugal at the expense of those of France. It did much to promote an already growing preference among the upper classes for stronger, more robust Peninsular wines. So much inferior wine was rushed to England in the years immediately following the treaty that demand initially fell. It rose sharply when shippers began to 'fortify' the wine for its journey by a judicious admixture of spirits. This was very different from the careful process subsequently developed, whereby the fermentation of fortified wines is arrested by the addition of brandy.

The Cat and Cucumber

When I was first commissioned in the army, I was stationed in Lancashire under a commanding officer who felt a deep sense of injury about being too old for action. He had as much interest in us, his subalterns, as I had in research into distemper. But fortunately he had a wife in whom the milk of human kindness flowed with abundance. As a result of her concern we were invited to have dinner, eight at a time;

had the old man had his way we would have been given cakes and ale in the drill hall, but he did not get his way. And so it was that one autumn evening, in the company of Second Lieutenants Fisher, Flint, Fosdyke, Freemantle, Freshwater, Fretwell and Fuller I walked down the Lancaster Road to the commanding officer's residence.

I don't remember too much about the meal other than that the Colonel's wife had asked the matron and a couple of elderly (anyone over 26 was elderly to us) nurses from

the local infirmary and while they did their best to make us feel at ease, we did our damnedest to get the staff to refill our glasses and drink the old boy into penury.

When the meal was over the ladies withdrew, the coffee arrived as did the port, and in the silence that ensued, one of my colleagues, Fretwell — who was slightly worldlier than the rest of us — said 'Very fine port, this sir. You know, they have excellent port at the Cat and Cucumber in Garstaing.' The Colonel looked at Fretwell for a long moment before he exploded — and in justification let me remind gentle readers who are too young or possibly too old, that this was a time when the average pub was lucky to have beer, let alone port-type wine, and the Cat and Cucumber in Garstaing was some way below being average. We listened while the old boy started off on the inadvisability of putting pearls before swine. 'Bloody little social upstarts' he went on. 'Always knew it was a mistake to have these bloody dinners. Now I know I was right. Mullery, take away the decanter. Gentlemen, you may piss off back to the barracks . . . and you sir will doubtless be going off to Garstaing.' We kicked Fretwell all the way back to the barracks — a man but for whom we would certainly have ended the night less sober than we were.

About fifteen years later I was at Lords watching a mid-week county match and while less than compulsive events occurred on the field of play, I went to the Long Room for a drink. There I found only one other occupant, the Colonel, older but still as angry and tetchy and intimidating as I remembered. He had been a County Cricketer, I was then a cricket writer for *The Observer*, and it seemed churlish not to make a gesture at conversation. The MCC is a Club, and that is what membership is all about, so I introduced myself. He nodded absently.

'I served under you in the Mixed Irish Brigade at Lancaster,' I said.

'Mmm?'

'You may recall, sir, that I had dinner with you when one of my colleagues compared your Croft's '24 to the hogwash they served at the Cat and Cucumber in Garstaing'.

The old boy suddenly came to life like a clockwork toy when you release the key. An arm swung. His mouth opened and closed. He blinked. His legs carried him a step away and then a step back. I watched with admiration. He finally regained his equanimity and said,

'Let me tell you something I've been wanting to tell someone for a very long time. After you had gone overseas I found that my batman had been selling my Cockburn's '29 to the local pub, and your chap was right.'

Port and liqueurs

Early 'port' was often fearsome stuff. By 1763, James Boswell was writing in his *London Journal*:

> *A bottle of thick English port is a very heavy and a very inflammatory dose. I felt it last time that I drank it for several days, and this morning it was boiling in my veins.*

The hangover had come a long way from Pepys' modest headache.

Hangovers were made even worse by the fashion for flavoured liqueurs, of which the future King George IV and his brothers were particularly fond; even in an age characterised by its broadmindedness a contemporary remarks upon the Prince Regent's habit of drinking cherry brandy 'in quantities not to be believed'. The Prince suffered appallingly from hangovers which, due to his indifference to servants' gossip, received a good deal of undesirable publicity; everyone knew that he used to alleviate them by bleeding, and would open the royal vein himself if his long-suffering physician refused to do it.

Gin

While the upper classes regaled themselves with fortified wines and liqueurs, gin replaced ale as the drink of the urban poor. The Dutch King William of Orange, who came to the throne in 1689, was not himself a heavy drinker, but his Dutch courtiers liked an occasional tot, and he naturally favoured a tariff system which gave preference to the spirits manufactured in his own native country. Gin rocketed in popularity partly because of its cheapness and partly because of the licensing laws, which at the beginning of the century allowed beer and cider to be sold only from licensed premises, but gin anywhere. In 1700 the annual consumption of gin amongst England's 5,000,000 people was estimated at 500,000 gallons; thirty-five years later it was eleven million — two million gallons more than it is today. By the time the authorities became convinced that something had to be done about the gin-shops the habit had taken too strong a hold to be effectively curtailed. The common name for gin was 'Blue Ruin'. A Victorian description of an East End tramp explains why:

> . . . *wonderful to relate, the face was perfectly blue —*
> *not indigo blue but of a ghostly, ghastly corpse-like*
> *kind of blue . . . That is gin.*
>
> Sir William Besant

Corpulence

The quantities of drink consumed during the eighteenth and early nineteenth centuries was matched, if not surpassed, by the amount of food considered necessary to sustain life among the better-off. Food has always been a status symbol, but never more so than at this period, when corpulence was not, as today, a source of shame and neurosis, but a pleasing indication of affluence and gentility. Gentlemen began the fashion of leaving the bottom waistcoat buttons undone, showing that the wearer was prosperous enough not to worry about filling the stomach beneath.

Patent medicines

Doctors and chemists realised that, just as there were fortunes to be made out of supplying food and drink, there were equal fortunes to be made from those suffering the after-effects. The Age of Indulgence was also the Age of the Patent Medicine. Chemists, free to sell anything that did not cause instant death (and that only because it was bad for business), dispensed their wares with hilarious abandon and a complete absence of official restraint on their advertising material. The Hangover Industry was born and the pillbox became a 'constant bedroom companion'.

Early eighteenth century doctors' remedies still relied on long-recognised herbal ingredients and were mainly purgatives, but during the latter part of the century the simple principle of ridding the body of alcoholic and other poisons as swiftly as possible gave way to a more subtle approach. The pursuit of the physician's El Dorado i.e. a sure-fire cure for gout (now achieved), led to more careful analysis of what actually went on in the stomach when it was bombarded with huge quantities of food and drink. As more became known about the chemical composition of the body and the acid-alkaline balance within it, so doctors and chemists devised cures by chemical correctives, usually alkaline preparations. Chemists made large claims for their products. A newspaper advertisement of 1785 for Stomachic Lozenges stated that they were a certain cure for:

> . . . most Disorders of the Stomach and Bowels, such as the Cholic and all Cholicy complaints, fixed Pains of the Stomach, Indigestion, Wind, Cold, Phlegm and Want of Appetite. They are excellent for expelling the Gout from the Stomach, and fixing it in the Feet or Hands, and immediately relieve those troublesome Consequences of a bad Digestion, a Fulness and Uneasiness after Eating, together with the Heart-burn, and all acid Crudities or Sour Risings and prevent the Ill Effects of hard Drinking, especially of bad wine, sour Punch, stale Beer, etc.

At 1s.6d. the box (about the same price as a bottle of port) they were a snip.

The Family Oracle of Health (1824) displays a nicely indulgent tone towards the hangover victim, though the actual prescription might not have resulted in so restful a 'morning after' as he suggests;

Feaster's morning Draught

> *Take two drachms of Rochelle salts,*
> *one ounce of infusion of senna,*
> *one teaspoonful of compound tincture of cardamons,*

54

*and (if you can get it) a small wine glass of Ratafia of
  Eau de Cologne*

*Mix, for a draught; and during the morning (after your
coffee, of course), take an occasional glass of strong
ginger beer. It will also be of great advantage to sit in a
snug fauteuil before a good fire, with your feet in
carpet shoes, planted comfortably on the hobs. This
position tends to keep the head erect, which is of the
utmost importance, while the warmth of the feet draws
the superabundance of blood downwards from the
brain, and consequently renders the nerves strong, the
spirits light, and the whole man cheerful and buoyant.*

Changing times

This kindly tone did not last. The more repulsive excesses
of the Prince Regent and his cronies probably helped to
turn public opinion against casual alcoholic over-indulgence,
and the increasing pace and pressure of life brought on by
the Industrial Revolution allowed less time for heavy
drinking and leisurely recovery. There was a distinct change
in attitude to drink during the nineteenth century,
particularly among the middle classes. Captain R. H.
Gronow, who fought with Wellington in the Peninsula and
whose drinking career began well before Waterloo (1815)
but lasted into the 1860s explains:

*There were then four, and even five-bottle men; and
the only thing that saved them was drinking very
slowly, and out of very small glasses. The learned head
of the law, Lord Eldon, and his brother Lord Stowell,
used to say that they had drunk more bad port than
any two men in England. The late Lords Panmure,*

55

Dufferin, and Blayney, wonderful to relate, were six-bottle men at this time; and I really think that if the good society of 1815 could appear before their more moderate descendents in the state they were generally reduced to after dinner, the moderns would pronounce their ancestors fit for nothing but bed.

Queen Victoria

Although the upper classes continued, as always, to drink and behave very much as they liked, a wind of change began to disperse the alcohol fumes from those who still had to preserve a reputation for respectability. The cult of gentility among the Victorians is always assumed to have been stimulated by the example of sober family life set by the Queen herself. Although no advocate of drunkenness, she was a violent opponent of teetotalism 'consenting to have one cleric promoted to a deanery only if he promised to stop advocating the pernicious heresy'. Her Highland servant John Brown preferred to take whisky rather than tea on their Scottish picnics, and one of her more endearing characteristics was her complete indifference to any reaction on the part of her other servants to the strong smell of whisky emanating from both Brown and herself on return. She also liked a measure of whisky mixed into her wine at meals, 'a concoction that startled Gladstone very much'.

There is of course no record of Queen Victoria suffering from a hangover but her cast-iron constitution would have been helpful in that respect. It may not have amused her to know how much of the hypocrisy that drove men to pubs and clubs and women to the private gin-bottle concealed under the bed is now ascribed to her influence.

Instant cures

Attitudes to hangovers and their cures changed with attitudes to drink. People tended to drink less openly and concealed their hangovers more. This led to the habit of trying to forestall the hangover by getting the alcohol out of the system even more quickly than it went in. 'Instant cures' for drunkenness became popular . . . all designed to bring the victim to his senses by short sharp shock, as often as not a powerful dose of ammonia. The violence of the prescriptions makes it quite clear that curing the affliction was of secondary concern to ensuring that the patient never again touched a drink. Doctors advised:

10 grains of sulphate of copper

half a drachm of sulphate of zinc or
five grains of tartar emetic

for clearing the body of alcohol; 'cures' that were likely to bring up half the patient's stomach as well as the contents thereof.

It was inevitable that sometimes a manufacturer would realise the commercial possibilities of a mixture on the lines of the home-made 'surfeit-waters' which had been distilled

by amateurs for centuries: an alcoholic base with a strong herbal flavouring. In 1844 Fernet Branca was released from the Fratelli Branca Distillerie in Milan to astound the drinking world and earn gold medals and Grand Diplomas from trade fairs in countries as far apart, gastronomically and geographically, as Brussels (1880) and Guatemala (1897), stopping to collect at Chicago (1893) on the way. No less could be expected from a drink which:

> . . . *promotes the flow of gastric juices and stimulates the involuntary muscles of the stomach. In this way it helps digestion and by its tonic action upon the intestines it helps assimilation of the nutriment and facilitates the elimination of bodily waste, thus increasing enormously your feeling of general well-being.*
>
> *Fernet Branca advertising hand-out*

Like all the best medicines, it can be drunk both before and after the party, and the next morning too. The same goes for Underberg, first marketed in 1846, containing selected herbs from forty-three countries, infused in a mixture of softened water and pure alcohol at a strength of 49% volume, slightly higher than the alcoholic strength of Fernet Branca. Underberg, still marketed by the family who originally devised the recipe, has enormous world-wide sales.

Coffee

For those who preferred non-alcoholic and non-medicinal cures, the eighteenth and nineteenth centuries had much to offer. Coffee, a benefit denied the Greeks and Romans, was prized for its effect on the hangover by the end of the seventeenth century, but it naturally had its opponents:

> *In a word, coffee is the drunkard's settle-brain, the fool's pastime, who admires it for being the production of Asia, and is ravished with delight when he hears the berries grow in the deserts of Arabia, but would not give a farthing for an hogshead of it, if it were to be had on Hampstead Heath . . .*
>
> > *T. Tryon,* The Good Housewife made a Doctor, *2nd ed. 1692*

Today doctors agree that it is not good for a hangover. It *seems* a help initially because it is a stimulant, but like drink itself, its diuretic properties make the dehydration worse if consumed in large quantities.

Tea

Those tempted to try tea as a substitute might be put off by the alarming conclusions of a Dr. Fernet:

> *Three or four cups of tea daily are by no means free from danger. The ill effects are due not only to the alkaloid it contains, but to the essential oil, which has a specially poisonous action. A single cup of tea may cause excitement and insomnia, while a stronger dose rarely fails to produce acute theism characterised by excitement, hyperaesthesia, palpitations, sweats and frequent micturation, and it may occasionally simulate Delirium Tremens.*

A favourite nineteenth century American remedy was milk toast, as was this 'Cordiall' from a Kansas Methodist recipe:

> *Mix one tablespoonful of cornstarch in one cup of good buttermilk, and heat but do not boil. Eat while hot like soup, with salt and pepper, or let cool and eat frequently, with plenty of honey for flavouring.*

Mineral waters

It is only fitting that Mr. Schweppe, an emigré Swiss living in London at the end of the eighteenth century, should have laid the foundations of his soft drinks empire by ministering to the afflictions of those devoted to hard liquor. Regency rakes soothed their hangovers with mineral waters, generally laced with a small quantity of spirits. One of the most famous, Lord Byron, was devoted to hock and soda-water, as was Oscar Wilde a century later. Contrary to popular belief, Lord Byron was not a very dedicated drinker. His writings reveal an engaging hypochondria!

> *. . . last night, I was prevailed upon . . . to swallow, at supper, a quantity of boiled cockles, and to dilute*

*them, not reluctantly, with some Imola wine. When I
came home, apprehensive of the consequences, I
swallowed three or four glasses of spirits, which men
(the vendors) call brandy, rum or Hollands, but which
Gods would entitle spirits of wine, coloured or sugared.
All was pretty well till I got into bed, when I became
somewhat swollen, and considerably vertiginous. I got
out, and mixing some soda-powders, drank them off.
This brought on temporary relief. I returned to bed;
but grew sick and sorry once again. Took more soda-
water. At last I fell into a dreary sleep. Woke, and was
ill all day, till I had galloped a few miles. Query: was it
the cockles, or what I took to correct them that caused
the commotion?*

There is something endearing about the Romantic Hero
with a hangover, especially as he is so vague as to the real
cause. Wordsworth, I suspect, would have blamed it
unhesitatingly upon the cockles, but then it is difficult to
imagine Wordsworth having a hangover at all, let alone
talking about one. The same is regrettably true of many
eminent Victorians; they may have suffered, but their
sufferings were for the most part endured in silence.

8

Heyday of the hangover

At the very beginning of this century the English-speaking effect of 'having consumed a surfeit of alcohol' acquired a name. It is difficult to assess why 'the hangover' chose exactly this moment to emerge from its twilight world and get itself included in dictionaries and the like; but King Edward VII might have had something to do with it. He had

made conviviality fashionable again at a court depressed by the long years of Queen Victoria's widowhood, but was the first to admit that a season's eating, drinking and late hours were bound to take their toll. Unlike George IV, who also suffered from the effects of over-sociability, he considered that leeches and laudanum were both messy and unsuited to the dignity of a monarch, and devised a far more elegant remedy: the annual migration to Biarritz or Baden-Baden where, in the company of congenial friends, fresh air and exercise could be enjoyed. Massage, Turkish baths and Spa waters were available for those who felt the need of them. The hangover cure had acquired style.

Spas

It was not, of course, a new idea in itself. Spas had been fashionable for years as refuges for the elderly and infirm; places where the young could try their social wings before fluttering into society and retreats to which they could return when their wings had been temporarily clipped by unrequited love or disaster in the card room. What was new was the attitude, hereby given the Royal seal of approval, that it was acceptable to admit that eating, and drinking and making merry had exhausting after-effects; that taking a cure involved no loss of face — something that had not been accepted since the time of the Romans.

Where the Regency bucks had pursued their pleasure with a feverish intensity and to hell with the consequences, the Edwardians ambled into enjoyment with open eyes. It was an era in which people finally began to call a spade a spade, and a hangover a hangover, though the new word did not come into popular usage until after the First World War.

Post-war decadence

The war changed everything. Social historians have tied themselves in sociological knots trying to analyse why the returning heroes of 1918 turned into the Bright Young Things of the 1920s. No-one has found a satisfactory answer. Whatever the cause, the effect was that pre-war it was enough simply to be smart, after the war it was smart to be decadent; drink has always been an indispensable accompaniment to decadence.

The easiest, certainly the cheapest way of implying that one has achieved the necessary degree of world weariness is to parade a hangover — so hangovers were in, especially in America where drink was out. A popular game of the time involved two people, each with a bottle of whisky and a glass. Both participants drink their whisky after which one goes out of the room, knocks on the door, and the other has to guess who it is.

Champagne

People drank, passed out, woke up and drank some more; they called it a cure, 'a hair of the dog'. In fact it was no more than a speedy return to the happy haze of the night before, made even speedier by glasses of Champagne which have the temperature and the bubbles to accelerate the process.

Champagne cocktails were especially in. Bucks Fizz, conceived as an Edwardian pick-me-up, consists of Champagne and fresh orange juice in proportions of about three to one. Black Velvet is Champagne and Guinness in equal quantities. N.B. Evelyn Waugh built upon the traditional Champagne Cocktail (sugar lump, three drops

angostura bitters, dessertspoonful brandy, 5 oz champagne) by first rolling his sugar lump in cayenne pepper.

Anything went and if you drank enough, the hangover went with it.

9

Cocktail cures

For a writer to plough into a chapter listing cocktails for
mornings after is like practising to sing a song for the deaf.
The victim of the hangover will grasp whatever is liquid with
gratitude; partly because it helps the dehydration, also
because it is good to feel your hand around a glass again,
and occasionally because it actually helps the malady.

The vogue for cocktails coincided with the era in which
hangovers became socially acceptable; there is no greater
connection than that. Nevertheless, there are more people
who can tell you the ingredients of a Bloody Mary or a
Prairie Oyster than know what goes into a Manhattan or a
Godfather.

Discipline v. indulgence

There are two distinct schools of thought, apart from the
hair of the dog syndrome.

1 Something to give you a sharp shock and persuade
   you to get an instant hold of yourself.

2 Some nursery concoction like a Banana Milk Shake
   made with one banana, a tablespoon of honey, and
   equal parts of milk and single cream, whizzed in a
   blender with four lumps of ice and strained into a tall
   glass.

The first method is disciplinary, the second indulgent. You must choose for yourself which approach is likely to have better results.

Bloody Mary

To my taste the very best Bloody Mary, is produced by mixing:

> ¼ *pint tomato juice*
> *1 dessertspoon Worcestershire sauce*
> *1 level coffeespoon celery salt*
> *1 dessertspoon fresh lemon juice*
> *6 drops Tabasco sauce*
> *1 generous measure single measure of vodka*
> *Stir in a cocktail glass with ice and strain*

In a Bullshot you use beef consommé instead of tomato juice.

Prairie oyster

The advantages of the Prairie Oyster type of pick-me-up is that it not only gives you a shock but it looks disgusting, tastes foul and has a vile consistency. The normal dose is one egg yolk in a glass anointed with tomato ketchup, Worcestershire sauce, cayenne pepper, chilli vinegar and rock-salt; occasionally brandy. Swallow it all in a gulp.

This is unhappily reminiscent of a story of my youth in which a woman of very limited means decided that she could save money on her weekly shopping trip if she took a bus to a nearby food-store instead of patronising the corner shop. Instead of the pleasant personal service to which she was used, she queued and asked, searched and waited, and finally, after one and a half hours emerged with the two eggs, yoghourt, ketchup, A.1. Sauce, and spare ribs she had set out to purchase. As she went to get on the bus home it started to move while she had only one foot on the platform and she fell, dropping her shopping which crashed to the pavement. As she sat among the broken debris sobbing bitterly, a nice woman saw her predicament and bent down to help her to her feet. 'Don't worry too much dear,' she said 'It wouldn't have lived, its eyes are too close together.' That, to me, is a Prairie Oyster.

A Prairie Hen, if you are still with me, is like the Oyster but you add the whole egg instead of just the yolk.

Pick-me-ups

As you now have the general idea of pick-me-ups let me simply add that barmen who know their jobs tend to alleviate the egregious taste of Fernet Branca with crème de menthe and balance the sweetness of that liqueur with brandy. Equal quantities of the three potions. Or for those who cannot face the egg, but still feel the stomach needs a salutary jolt:

> Old Pepper
> *1 jigger whisky*
> *Juice of ½ a lemon*
> *1 teaspoon Worcestershire sauce*
> *1 teaspoon chilli sauce or*
> *1 tablespoon tomato juice*
> *2 or 3 dashes angostura*
> *1 dash Tabasco*

Mix thoroughly.
David Embury: The Fine Art of Mixing Drinks

Milk and Honey

Milk settles the stomach, and honey keeps up the blood sugar level, and the alcohol presumably does something or other, but I include the following from a sense of duty rather than a prospect of pleasure:

> Hair of the Dog
> 1 oz.   scotch
> 1½ oz. heavy cream
> 1½ oz. honey

Shake vigorously (if you can stand the noise) with shaved ice and serve.
John Doxat: Booths Handbook of Cocktails
and Mixed Drinks

Corpse-Revivers

The reviving here is done entirely by the alcohol, of which one-third is generally a type with 'medicinal' properties, such as Fernet Branca or absinthe (use Pernod or Anis):

> The Savoy Hotel's Corpse-Reviver
> ⅓ *brandy*
> ⅓ *Fernet Branca*
> ⅓ *white crême de menthe*

Shake with ice, strain and serve.
Booths Handbook

71

The 'Jeeves' Cocktail Book Corpse-Reviver
⅓ *sweet vermouth*
⅓ *calvados*
⅓ *brandy*

Stir and strain into a glass.

Exotica

These are for the lunchtime drinker who wishes to advertise a hangover rather than seek relief for a genuine indisposition.

Morning Glory Fizz
2 teaspoons sugar syrup
Juice of ½ lime
Juice of ½ lemon
1 egg white
1 pony absinthe
1 jigger scotch

Shake all the ingredients together with crushed ice (insist on its being crushed very small), strain into a large glass and top up with 1½ oz. soda water (make sure this is measured exactly, especially if produced from a siphon).

David Embury: The Fine Art of Mixing Drinks

For real weaklings there is:

The Bromo Seltzer
In a tumbler place:
2 teaspoons Bromo Seltzer
3 drops aromatic spirits of ammonia

*Half fill a second tumbler with soda and plain water.
Mix by pouring contents from one glass to another, and
serve.*

*(N.B. Bromo is not particularly common nowadays, but
Enos Liver Salts, etc., would have the same effect.)*

Personally I find that reassuring cures are very much more
effective than those hell-bent on removing the back of your
throat, though I can see the point. I once went to a doctor
after a particularly convivial evening, he asked me to show
him my tongue and after taking a quick look he said, 'If I
were you, I wouldn't put that back in your mouth'.

Morning after food

A plate of Grape Nuts with soft brown sugar and cold gold
top milk is a good base on which to build a new stomach the
morning after. The Irish swear by mashed potatoes. A glass
of cold milk and Perrier water is helpful. Porridge with salt
and cream acts like an insulating layer between what went
on and what is going to occur. The trouble is that the sub-
porridge mass will not like it.

There are people who swear by jelly. Just give me a nice
plate of raspberry jelly and custard, they say, and I will feel as
right as rain. These folk may well be right in what they say;
on the other hand I seriously doubt whether they had a
hangover, because nothing that you take after a really
substantial drinking bout can, will or should make you feel
that good.

10

In vino veritas

Baulked of an instant physical cure, it might be most sensible to concentrate on the best mental attitude to adopt, if only to pass the time while the Alka Seltzer dissolves.

Indifference

Ignore the hangover. Remember that Tony Benn, Mrs Pankhurst, Genghis Khan, Attila the Hun, Ralph Nader and the Bionic Man never had a hangover, so why should you? You are probably sickening for something. Make a medical appointment with a busy doctor.

'You look ill!'

'I am seeing my doctor next week', always sounds convincing.

Analysis

See your hangover for what it is, a collection of temporary ills each one of which can be individually cured. By the time you have ministered to a third of them the rest will have gone. Eschew feelings of guilt, they tend to last longest. Remember the early nineteenth-century bon viveur Sydney Smith:

> *I start up at two o'clock in the morning, after my first sleep, in an agony of terror, and feel all the weight of*

life upon my soul. It is impossible that I can bring up
such a family of children, my sons and daughters will
be beggars; I shall live to see those whom I love
exposed to the scorn and contumely of the world! But
stop, thou child of sorrow, and humble imitator of Job,
and tell me on what you dined. Was there not soup
and salmon, and then a plate of beef, and then duck,
blanc-mange, cream cheese, diluted with beer, claret,
champagne, hock, tea, coffee and noyeau? And after
all this, you talk of the mind and the evils of life? These
kind of cases do not need meditation, but magnesia.

Comparison

There are others in the same state. Ring them and discuss
how they feel. Remember those who behaved worse than
you (there must be someone). Go to the churchyard of
St. Bartholomew's in the City of London and look at the
meths drinkers. Read the *Times* obituary. Try G. K.
Chesterton:

> *But Noah he sinned and we have sinned; on tipsy feet*
>   *we trod,*
> *Till a great big black Teetotaller was sent to us for a*
>   *rod.*
> *And you can't get wine at a PSA or a chapel or*
>   *Eisteddfod*
> *For the curse of water has come again because of the*
>   *wrath of God,*
> *And water is on the Bishop's Board and the Higher*
>   *Thinker's shrine*
> *But I don't care where the water goes if it doesn't get*
>   *into the wine.*

Read Kingsley Amis' *Lucky Jim*:

> *Dixon was alive again. He lay sprawled, too wicked to move, spewed up like a broken spider-crab on the tarry shingle of the morning. The light did him harm, but not as much as looking at things did; he resolved, having done it once, never to move his eyeballs again. A dusty thudding in his head made the scene before him beat like a pulse. His mouth had been used as a latrine by some small creature of the night, and then as its mausoleum. During the night, too, he'd somehow been on a cross-country run and then been expertly beaten up by secret police. He felt bad.*

Disguise

This is only recommended for people possessing great powers of cunning and concentration.

The only effective form of hangover disguise is long-term, and requires forethought. It is based on the formula long in use by judges who have constantly to fight the accusation that they fall asleep on the bench. The trick is to pretend to be asleep *all the time.* A couple of brisk verbal interjections per hour in the intervals of genuine peaceful slumber are enough to gain a reputation for vast judicial wisdom and wiliness. Why should it not be the same with the hangover? A convincing moan after a not-too-taxing evening, followed by equally convincing evidence of lightning recovery leaves the field clear for undisturbed rumination during a really bad attack because no-one will ever call your bluff again.

The late, great actor Wilfred Lawson was a brilliant proponent. Starting out on a session he gave every impression that he had drunk almost exactly the amount he was going to drink, so that he spent the time establishing the physical norm for which he had mentally prepared himself, and you.

Curriculum vinae

In the hotel industry in which I served an apprenticeship, and which trade I pursued for much of my working life — perhaps for all of my working life — we knew that a man who was mean when he was drunk was a dangerous customer. If I were a headhunter, the variety which recruits senior management, I would go far less on the recommend-ation of headmaster, college tutor or employer, than on that of local publican or hotel barman. He knows. No-one succeeds in pulling rank in the pub or bar, and the professional opinion of one who has seen you before, after and during a hard night's consumption, is something of which careful note should be taken.

Gilbert Harding

In the 1950s the late Gilbert Harding, who knew much about the inside of bottles, achieved great fame and fortune by being himself on television and radio. He was, for those who do not date to that era, a blend between an angry Magnus Pyke and an academic Barbara Woodhouse.

During his humbler years he had drunk at The Stag in New Cavendish Street, a popular BBC pub much frequented by Features producers who were easy to recognise by their dandruff. (Rumour had it that the Head of Features had a

daily roll-call at which he shook dandruff over the jackets of his staff).

There came a time when the manager of The Stag had done well enough for himself to buy his own Free House in the Home Counties. He asked Gilbert Harding if he would come and preside at the opening ceremonies of his new establishment and the great man, who was as generous as he was intolerant, said he would be honoured to do so. Gilbert arrived in his chauffeur-driven car, smiled at the photographers of the local newspapers, pulled the first pint, made a short and witty speech and remained for a while, drinking and chatting. About half a bottle later, he went up to the bar, squinted at the wife of the ex-Stag landlord and said, 'D'ye know you are one of the ugliest bitches I've seen for many a long day' and flicked the content of his glass in her face.

Pandemonium.

She shouted, the crowd milled. The chauffeur plunged to the rescue. A shamed Harding was bundled into his vehicle and departed to the boos of the local populace.

Absolutely overcome with remorse Gilbert Harding sent the landlady a huge bouquet of flowers, and a grovelling letter of apology. A year to the day after the opening he came, by arrangement, to the Home Counties Pub to wish them well on the first anniversary of their enterprise and pledge his friendship. He was welcomed, made much of, delivered a short speech, chatted and drank, and sometime before they muscled him out of the place for the second and final time, he had gone up to the landlady, flicked his drink in her face and said, 'I washright; you're a bloody ugly bitch'.

In conclusion

It will come as a disappointment (and a blow if you are the sort of sober swine who starts a book at the end to see what there is in it for you) to conclude that there is no satisfactory remedy for the ailment.

While I have discussed the wisdom of practising moderation in all things, it is not what I preach.

Half a sixpence may be better than no money at all. Half

a hangover merely wrecks the night before as well as the morning after. Lord Byron put it succinctly:

Let us have wine and women, mirth and laughter . . .
Sermons and Soda Water the day after.

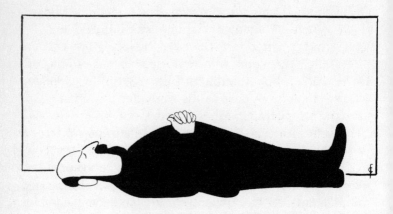